How To Have A Successful Product Manager Career

The Things That You Need To Be Doing TODAY In Order To Have A Successful Product Manager Career

"Practical, proven techniques that will help you to have a successful product manager career"

Dr. Jim Anderson

Published by:
Blue Elephant Consulting
Tampa, Florida

Library of Congress Control Number: 2013952526

ISBN-13: 978-1493515073

ISBN-10: 1493515071

Warning – Disclaimer

The purpose of this book is to educate and entertain. This book does not promise or guarantee that anyone following the ideas, tips, suggestions, techniques or strategies will be successful. The author, publisher and distributor(s) shall have neither liability nor responsibility to anyone with respect to any loss or damage caused, or alleged to be caused, directly or indirectly by the information contained in this book.

Acknowledgements

Any book like this one is the result of years of real-world work experience. In my over 25 years of working for 7 different firms, I have met countless fantastic people and I've been mentored by some truly exceptional ones. Although I've probably forgotten some of the people who made me the person that I am today, here is my attempt to finally give them the recognition that they so truly deserve:

- Thomas P. Anderson
- Art Puett
- Bobbi Marshall
- Bob Boggs

Dr. Jim Anderson

This book is dedicated to my wife Lori. None of this would have been possible without her love and support.

Thanks for the best 21 years of my life (so far)...!

Speaking.　Negotiating.　Managing.　Marketing.

Table Of Contents

What's The Best Way To Start?

Congratulations – you are a product manager. Or you want to be one. No matter where your career is at right now, what we need to have a talk about is how you can take it to the next level.

Being a product manager is a strange sort of job. It turns out that you don't actually "do" anything. Instead, it's your job to get a lot of other people to do all of the things that are going to be required in order to make a product or a group of products be successful.

Needless to say this is a hard thing to do. However, as hard as that is, there is something else that you need to be doing at the same time: managing your career. Look, the success of your product is never only in your hands. Market conditions, what your competition does, and the whims of your customers will all conspire to either make your product a success or a flop.

No matter what the final result is, and often we don't even get to stick around for the last chapter, you are going to want your efforts today to move your career forward tomorrow.

What this means for you is that you need to understand what it is going to take to get the rest of your company to recognize the good work that you are doing today and the potential that you have for tomorrow. The good news is that this can be easily done. You just have to know how.

Product managers can get caught up in the details of their product. There always seem to be new requirements to create, product launches to schedule, and features to document. However, the secret to being a successful product manager is to realize that the job is really about having good communication skills. It's the people that you work with both inside of your company as well as outside of your company that will determine how far you'll go in your career.

This book has been written to give you a helping hand. I want to get you to take notice of the day-to-day things that are going to play a role in determining the next step in your career. It's not going to be your technical knowledge or your understanding of your market that is going to help you to move to the next level, but rather how others perceive you.

Contained in this book are the tips and tricks that you are going to need in order to take control of your product manager career. As you read each chapter, take a moment to think about how you can start to use the information in your job immediately. I think that you are going to be both surprised and pleased with just how much this information is going to help you take your product manager career to the next level!

Good luck!

-    Dr. Jim Anderson, October, 2013

About The Author

I must confess that I never set out to be a product manager. When I went to school, I studied Computer Science and thought that I'd get a nice job programming and that would be that. Well, at least part of that plan worked out!

My first job was working for Boeing on their F/A-18 fighter jet program. I spent my days programming fighter jet software in assembly language and I loved it. The U.S. government decided to save some money and went looking for other countries to sell this plane to. This put me into an unfamiliar role: I started to meet with foreign military officials in order to explain what my product did.

Time moved on and so did I. I found myself working for Siemens, the big German telecommunications company. They were making phone switches and selling them to the seven U.S. phone companies. The problem was that the switches were too complicated. Customers couldn't tell the difference between one complicated phone switch from another complicated phone switch.

The Siemens sales folks were in a bind. They didn't know enough about how the switches worked to tell their customers why they should buy them. Siemens reached out into their engineering unit looking for anyone who could help the sales teams out. I put my hand up and overnight I became a product manager.

Since then I've spent over 20 years working as a product manager for both big companies and startups. This has given me an opportunity to do everything that a product manager does many, many times. I know what works as well as what doesn't work.

I now live in Tampa Florida where I spend my time managing my consulting business, Blue Elephant Consulting, teaching college courses at the University of South Florida, and traveling to work with companies like yours to share the knowledge that I have about how product managers can make their product be a success.

I'm always available to answer questions and I can be reached at:

Dr. Jim Anderson
Blue Elephant Consulting
Email: jim@BlueElephantConsulting.com
Facebook: http://goo.gl/1TVoK
Web: http://www.BlueElephantConsulting.com/

"Unforgettable communication skills that will set your ideas free..."

Create Products Your Customers Want At A Price That They Are Willing To Pay!

Dr. Jim Anderson is available to provide training and coaching on the two topics that are the most important to product managers everywhere: how do I create the products that my customers want and what should I price them at?

Dr. Anderson believes that in order to both learn and remember what he says, product managers need to laugh. Each one of his speeches is full of fun and humor so that what he says "sticks" with everyone.

Dr. Anderson's Product Management Training Includes:

1. How can you segment your market?
2. What problems are your customers having right now?
3. Which of your customer's problems does your product solve?
4. How much of this problem does your product solve?
5. How much will it cost your customer if they don't fix this problem?

Dr. Jim Anderson presents over 100 speeches per year. To invite Dr. Anderson to speak at your event, contact him at:

Phone: 813-418-6970 or
Email: jim@BlueElephantConsulting.com

Blue
Elephant
Consulting

Speaking. Negotiating. Managing. Marketing.

Chapter 1

Why Can't Product Managers Get Any Respect?

Why Can't Product Mangers Get Any Respect?

Let's look at the "respect pyramid" that, although unofficial, exists in nearly every organization. If we start at the top, then we find the Subject Matter Experts (SMEs) who are the people who really know what's going on both in the company and with the technology. These are the people who make sure that the team is really solving the right problem: *"That won't work because that's not the way that we take orders for that product..."*

Just under them you'll find the legacy crew — those folks who have been working on a system or a technology longer than anyone else and are the ones that everyone goes to in order to solve technology problems.

Beneath them you will find the code rockets. These are the folks who have an amazing ability to turn out code or other productive work seemingly overnight. When a schedule gets tight, they are the ones to turn to.

Once you get this far down on the respect pyramid, things get a bit boring. That is until you get to the bottom. I've got good news for the Product Management world; we're not at the bottom. I truly believe that the bottom of the respect pyramid is reserved for the good souls who work on the Quality Assurance (QA) team.

Just above them (doing better, but not by much) are the Program Managers. The bad news is the Product Managers sit just above Program Managers which is way too close to the bottom of the pyramid if you ask me.

This, of course, begs the question: why? How did Product Mangers come to live so close to the bottom of the respect pyramid? If you take a look at who is up at the top, you'll notice something very interesting: the most respected people in an organization are givers, not takers. Sure there are exceptions to every rule, but this is most often the case. Way down at the bottom of the respect pyramid you find the folks who are viewed (rightly or wrongly) as basically being takers, not givers.

This sad realization generates the question: so what can be done to improve the lot of Product Mangers? Clearly Product Managers need to find a way to be seen as givers. So what do we have to give?

The three quick answers that come to mind are direction, status, and understanding. Direction has to do with making sure that the product team knows what they are working on and what problem it is designed to solve.

Status means making sure that every member of the team fully understands at all times how the product is coming along and what the outside world thinks about the product team. Please note that an occasional "Status" email does not even come close to accomplishing this goal.

Understanding is the most important and the most difficult to do. The product team lives an insulated life and often times do not understand why certain decisions are made or why the team or the product is viewed as it is. It is the Product Manger's responsibility to monitor all of these things and relay them back to the team in terms that they can understand.

Chapter 2

People or Products –
Which Do You Mange
Better?

People or Products –
Which Do You Mange Better?

Nobody ever said that being a product manager was going to be easy, and I think that we can all agree that it's a tough job. There's been a lot of talk about finding a way to certify product managers by making them go back to school; however, I think that at the heart of the task is the need to achieve a balance between the product and the people working on it.

No, we're not CEOs of the company, however we are ultimately CEOs of our products and too many of us view our organizations as being either product or people focused.

Look, we are all under a great deal of pressure all of the time. Our budgets are too small to begin with and will get cut even further when the company runs into a tough quarter, people leave the project, other departments don't want to work with us, and don't even get me started on outside vendors and suppliers.

Yet, still we are ultimately responsible for fixing problems and creating and delivering a successful product. I will confess that when I've been handed a new product to manage, I have the habit of quickly scoping my vision down to the product – what needs to be done to make it successful, people be damned.

Russell Eisenstat is a former Harvard Business School prof has been studying CEOs who do a good job of balancing the product / people scale correctly. There is a great deal that product managers can learn from Russell's work. What would any effort be worth if there wasn't a clever acronym and so Russell has come up with the term HCHP which refers to "High-Commitment and High-Performance" firms & leaders.

So here's the question that we product managers need to find an answer to: how are successful leaders able to resolve the necessary tensions that exist between their quest for creating profitable products and their desire to build a sustainable team that has a high-commitment level?

As a product manager I personally feel that I'm motivated by something much deeper than short term profits. I feel a sense of responsibility to leave the company in a better position than I found it. This means creating a successful product AND creating a successful team.

Chapter 3

People Product Managers Under Pressure

People Product Managers Under Pressure

As a product manager, we are really under incredible daily pressure to meet the performance demands of our investors. All too often we don't view our upper managers as investors; however, at the end of the day that is really what they are.

They have decided to spend money on our product and not something else so clearly they expect our product to produce a return that is larger than the other options could have provided. If you don't meet this need, then give it up – nothing else really matters.

How can you push for the superior performance that will be required in order to meet your management's expectations? In many cases you'll be called on to make extraordinary decisions and even implement unconventional ideas. One example of this would be recommending that your product be killed if you came to realize that it had no hope of being successful. How many product managers that you know would have the guts to do that?

Having the courage to make big decisions is great; however, it means nothing if you take the commitment of your team for granted and end up having your decisions destroy the delicate social fabric that holds your organization together. Really good Product Managers find a way to personally create a link between the people who are doing the work and the results that they must deliver.

I can hear you now saying "great words, but how do I do that...?" You do it by simultaneously combining four different strategies that will allow you to hold the center and not stray off course:

- **Earn Trust**: Product Managers need to earn the trust of everyone who is working on their product. The ONLY way to do this is to be open with your team and to always share the truth with them – get caught in one lie or half-truth and the game is over.

- **Engage Deeply**: Build a close connection with everyone on your team so that when you interact with them it can be direct and personal.

- **Create a Focused Agenda**: In order to mobilize a group of people, a Product Manager needs to have a very clearly defined and focused agenda that can be communicated and bought into by the entire team.

- **Build Leadership**: a Product Manager cannot be everywhere at all times nor can he/she do everything. This means that the Product Manager needs to be building a leadership team within the product team so that progress can continue even when the Product Manager is not available.

In order to pull this off you are going to have to create a sense of shared purpose for your team. Nobody ever said that this product management job was going to be easy!

Chapter 4

How Great Product Managers Keep Their Perspective

How Great Product Managers Keep Their Perspective

There are a lot of Product Managers in the world. The question is what makes some of them great product managers? We've been talking about high-commitment, high-performance product (HCHP) product managers and they are truly the great ones. What makes these product managers better than all of the rest is that they have found a way to keep their work in perspective and this is what makes all the difference. So what's their secret?

The first secret to keeping perspective is that great product managers find a way to stay close with their teams while at the same time maintaining a distance. What this means is that everyone on the team feels as though they know the product manager and that he/she knows them. At the same time, we all know that sometimes difficult staffing decisions need to be made and keeping a distance allows the great product managers to not be accused of playing favorites.

Secondly, great product managers actually have a life outside of work. No matter if it is just spending time with their families or throwing themselves into a hobby that they truly enjoy, they find a way to make sure that their job is not all that there is to life. This helps them to maintain a perspective about the job.

Finally, humor always helps. The great product managers are able to laugh at themselves and their situation. This ability can relieve tension that would otherwise spill over and poison workplace relationships. Additionally, when a product manager shows that he/she can laugh at themselves, then the entire team feels more relaxed around them and the team will function more smoothly.

Ultimately, a great product manager achieves that status not by **WHAT** they do, we all know what we are supposed to be doing, but rather **HOW** they do things. Great product mangers realize that the profession of product management is really a calling, not a science and it can only be done well by someone using their artistic talent, not their engineering skills.

Chapter 5

Should You Get An MBA?

Should You Get An MBA?

I had a chance to talk with one of my friends the other day who is a product manager working in the telcom space. Carol is basically happy with her job, but she's tired of always gathering requirements and she is already starting to think about the next step in her career – becoming a Director. She told me that she was thinking about getting an MBA; however, she had not made up her mind yet as to if it would be worth the time, energy, and expense required to get one. She wanted to know what I thought?

Just a little background info for you here: I've collected four university degrees. I've got a BS, MS, and PhD in Computer Science and then I went on and just for good measure I picked up an MBA with a focus on Marketing. All in all this took me about 15 years to do. Because of the time, energy, and expense that I've gone through I felt that Carol was talking to the right person!

The first thing that I asked Carol was where she wanted to take her career and what she thought that she needed to do to get there (besides getting an MBA). She said that she had been doing some studying of the last four or five IT people who had been promoted to a Director position.

What she had found that they had all been at the company for at least 5 years, they had been associated with a successful project, they were well known to the Executive Director that they would be reporting to. She then said that only two of the five new Directors had an MBA – the other three had at least a Masters technical degree.

Carol had done her homework! We then spent some time talking about what you can expect to get if you get an MBA. Assuming that you can't take time off from your job to go to school for two years, then you are probably looking at going to night school for 4-5 years.

I realize that there are other options such as the University of Phoenix and Executive MBA programs; however, my experience has been with the traditional butt-in-a-classroom-at-night approach. One of the first questions that I asked Carol was if she expected to be living where she was right now for the next 5 years – nothing could be sadder than moving half-way through a program! Carol said that yes, she expected to be in town for the next 5 years.

I got my MBA for two reasons: I wanted to have the vocabulary that was needed to work with the people who are running the business and I wanted to network with other people who were at the same stage of their career as I was. In the end, I feel that I got the vocabulary that I wanted. A lot of that vocabulary has to do with finance, organizational behavior, and marketing and these had been things that I didn't know much about before starting my MBA.

The networking with other folks who were working on their MBA didn't work out as well. When one attends the big Ivy League schools to get an MBA, you have the advantage of moving through your courses with your peers in lock step.

The MBA program that I was in had more people in it and so we were spread out both over time (some people completed in 3 years, some took as long as 7 years) and in courses – there were a lot of courses offered each semester. This meant that few close relationships were formed that lasted more than a semester or two.

In my case I moved out of town after completing the degree and so the value of the networking was even more minimized. All that being said, I believe that if you went into the program with networking as a key goal, you could build up a healthy LinkedIn network by the time you were though.

The final benefit of getting an MBA is that you get a chance to be exposed to a great deal of business information that you may have heard of, but never had a chance to study before.

Depending on what your background is, this material may be very straightforward.

Unlike technical degrees, an MBA requires you to work in teams, give in-class presentations and really doesn't have that many problem sets to turn in. Rather, questions require wordy answers – you have to memorize a great deal of information that does not have a formula or numbers associated with it. I found the studying to be easy because it was all new. It kept my interest and was easy to memorize.

After I had shared all of this with Carol, she decided to go ahead and take the GMAT in order to apply to enter an MBA program. What helped her to finally make her mind up is that she took a look at the people who would be her competition for the next Director position and decided that an MBA would set her apart from them.

Chapter 6

The #1 Skill That A Product Manager Needs To Have

The #1 Skill That A Product Manager Needs To Have

Yes, I will tell you what this skill is; however, do you think that you can guess it before I do? I'm sure that you can come up with the standard list of leadership skills that every product manager has (or at least should have): able to deal with pressure, able to lead people, vision, positive attitude, creativity, etc.

However, those would all be good to have, but none of them would be the #1 skill that a product manager needs to have. Give up? The answer is ...

Good Judgment.

The ability to make good decisions is the #1 skill that any product manager needs to have because making decisions is such a large part of what we do each and every day. Two well-known business thinkers / authors also agree with me: Noel Tichy and Warren Bennis.

Noel and Warren say that judgment can be broken up into three different sets of skills: picking who will be on your team (people), picking what challenges you take on (strategy), and picking what to do when tough times hit (crisis decisions).

People, people, people. Decisions about which people a product manger is going to interact with and have on his / her team are **THE** most important decisions that they will ever make.

Don't believe me? Then maybe you'll believe Jack Welsh who said that the thing that he failed at the most during his storied career was moving too slowly in making people judgments even when he had all of the data that he needed.

Tichy reports that when he's giving speeches he'll ask the audience what the worse judgment that they every made was and invariably about 75% of the people will say that they were about people. If a product manager can get the right people on his / her team, then they have solved more than half of the problem.

Next comes what product strategy a product manager wants to pursue. In our world, more often than not this comes down to picking what types of customers we want to go after with our products.

Our sales teams are all too often filled with salespeople who will happily go after every customer that they can get a meeting with. However, this is a great way to waste time until all of the money is gone. Picking the right customers from the get-go and going after them aggressively is what a good product manager makes happen.

Bad things happen and a product manager who is ready for them is a product manager who has real-world survival skills. When the whole world seems to have flipped upside down (like when the stock market drops 700 points in a single day!), a product manager who can remain calm and still make good decisions is worth his/her weight in gold.

Now this ability is probably as much an art as it is a science; however, at the end of the day it always requires that the product manager know all of the available facts about the situation. To put it simply, the ability to collect the facts is one of the simple secrets behind a product manager's ability to make good judgments.

Chapter 7

How Product Managers Can Make Time Work For Them

How Product Managers Can Make Time Work For Them

Dang – just where does the time seem to go? I don't know about you but as of late I seem to be running out of time or just simply running behind more often than in the past. I'd like to blame the current turmoil in the financial markets; however, that's not the problem.

There are many, many more people who are better qualified than I talk about time management (I'm sorta a fan of GTD myself), but I do have one secret that I'd like to share with you. No promises, but if you believe what I'm going to share with you and if you take the time to implement it, then there is a pretty good chance that you'll become the best product manager in the world. Sound interesting? Then read on...

Forget having enough time to do everything that you have to get done. Instead, think for just a moment about projecting an image of being in control of your time. What do you think would happen if everyone who encountered you was left with the impression that you had it all under control?

Would your boss be impressed? Would your team be more willing to do what you tell them to do? Could you run meeting more efficiently? Would you just get more respect from everyone? You may be laughing right now and saying that a thin veneer of control put over your normal out-of-control personality is not going to accomplish anything. However, that's where I think that you would be wrong...

If you think back a bit, you might remember that there was a book called The Secret that was very popular a while ago. In a nutshell, the secret was that if you can imagine something, then you can make it happen. This applies to making others believe that you have control over your time. However, I'm going get just a bit more specific here and give you one single change that if you implement it will have a dramatic and positive impact on your life: start showing up early.

What this means in the day-to-day life of a product manager is that you need to start to show up for meeting early (5-10 minutes will do) and even more importantly, you need to start to jump on call bridges early (5 minutes will do here).

I don't know about you, but up until just recently I was a constantly late shower-upper. I would slide into calls 5 minutes late and hope that whoever was running the meeting would not stop the call and ask who had just joined when they heard the "beep" that announced my arrival. I'd slug through the call and then slink off when it was over no better or worse for the time spent on the call.

A few weeks ago, I accidentally showed up for a call early. You can imagine how surprised I was when there was nobody on the bridge when I joined (there was that moment where I felt that I needed to check to make sure that I had the right call-in numbers). What happened next really caught my attention: other people started to join.

These just happened to be people that I had been trying with no luck to get in touch with. I had very quick, very short conversations with three of them as they joined and got commitments from them to send me answers and materials that I desperately needed. As others joined I exchanged small talk with them and reconnected with people that I knew but had not seen in a long time.

When the call's leader joined he fumbled around for a bit and this gave me time to ask a very good, penetrating question about what he wanted to accomplish on this call and that got everyone involved in a discussion. Man, it was almost like I was running the show!

Based on the success of this accidental event, I started showing up early for all of my meetings that week and found that the same sequence of events repeated itself. Others looked at me as though I was in charge, I connected with other people who were in the meeting, and I was able to make face-to-face requests for support and materials that were never turned down. Wow – who knew that getting what you wanted could be so easy?

Yes, I realize that showing up early for meetings and calls won't solve all of life's problems. However, it sure seems to make a lot of little things run much easier. When you couple that with the fact that it's so very easy to do, why not give it a try and see what it does for you?

Chapter 8

How To Jump-Start A Stalled Product Manager

How To Jump-Start A Stalled Product Manager

Ugh! The financial world seems to be going to hell-in-a-hand-basket, a global recession appears to either be here or be looming, Microsoft's latest operating system is still a dog, and all of those political TV commercials have now officially become annoying. Being a product manager is a tough job on the best of days, but it sure seems like right now it can be a real challenge to even get out of bed let alone be the #1 cheerleader for your product. What's a product manager to do?

If you were a car sitting in the parking lot at work, your dome light wouldn't even turn on when a door was opened – that's how low your energy level is right now. What you need is a good, swift kick in the … , oh wait, that's for later. Right now what you need is a jump-start. What you need is guidance from the world famous motivational speaker Brian Tracy to get you pointed in the right direction in order to get you off of your butt and back on track:

1. **Everyone Needs An Action Plan:** Come on and admit it – you love plans. Write down everything that you need to be doing and then go back and put an A (high priority), B, or C (low priority) next to each one of them. Brian says that "… a written plan leads you into action." How's that for getting started?

2. **Get Yourself Clean:** No, we're not talking about drugs (but you probably should do something about that also), rather we're talking about your work area. What would your mom say if she saw it right now? This is busy work that won't take too much of your gray matter to quickly make better – do it and then feel happy about it.

3. **Two Buckets: Urgent vs. Important:** You've probably heard this one before, but you can't hear it too many

times. The urgent stuff needs your attention right now – get on it. The important stuff will need your attention, but it can wait just a bit.

4. **Go For The Big Value:** Those big projects scare all of us – where to start? It really doesn't matter, just start. You need to tackle the big important tasks that will have a long term payoff for you first. Yeah, yeah, I know that you'd like to get some quick wins by starting with some little tasks, but don't. Time will fly by and the big boys will still be there and you'll be even farther behind.

5. **Procrastinate!:** Yes, you really should do this! The trick is making sure that you procrastinate on the tasks that will contribute little or nothing to accomplishing your really big goals. Keep pushing them off and I'll bet that you'll find that they end up fading away...

We all get burned out, run down, or just simply run out of gas. The key point is to quickly realize that this has happened and to do something about it. Even the best product managers have their off days. The next time that you find yourself staring at the ceiling, whip out this list and get back to work!

Chapter 9

How To Keep Your Product Manager Job In A Recession

How To Keep Your Product Manager Job In A Recession

If you are a product manager at one of the big 3 car makers or even if you work for the company formally known as Motorola, times cannot be good for you right now. The rest of us are also looking over our shoulders trying to figure out if our jobs might be on the chopping block next.

Every Product Manger would like to think that he/she is so valuable to the company that there is **NO WAY** that their name would ever get put on the RIF list. However, I speak from experience when I say – it happens! So perhaps the big question is really, is there anything that you can do to get yourself spared the axe? Well, it turns out that the answer is maybe...

Look, if the company is shutting down, then you are out of a job no matter what. However, if they are going to keep going, then you have a chance to hold on to your job. Now, there are no guarantees, but you can improve your odds product manager by doing the following things:

- **Look Like You Are A Survivor**: Interestingly enough, you want to do this because it's much easier to can someone who looks like they have already been canned. This means that you've got to lighten up – don't drag around all moody like. Research has shown that if you are fun to be around, people will want to be around you especially in bad times. Good natured colleagues are chosen over ones in a bad mood and that's always a good thing.

- **Become A Beacon Of Hope:** People often survive when they do things that others don't do. You need to realize that upper management is feeling the downturn just as much as anyone else, and maybe even more if a large part of their salary is based on their bonus. If you become upbeat and don't fight the changes that come your way, then you will be seen as a leader and as an advocate that upper management can rely on. Once again, this is a very good thing.

- **Practice Good Citizenship:** In good times, we hate to go to those big meetings, all hands meetings, etc. Who needs the pep rally; I've got real work to do. However, when times are tough, you need to start attending all of these meetings. Become visible – make sure that everyone knows that you are going, that you are there, and that you are a supporter of the message that is being delivered.

You don't have control over the future of you company nor do you really have control over your career's future – you're pretty much just along for the ride. However, that doesn't mean that you can't try to tip the odds in your favor.

Sometimes just buying yourself just a bit more time can make all the difference in the world. Hanging on until the bad times are just about over will make finding that next product manager gig that much easier!

Chapter 10

Are Executive MBAs Valuable To Product Mangers?

Are Executive MBAs Valuable To Product Mangers?

As the world's economy continues to shudder, everyone is scrambling to find ways to make themselves more valuable to both their current employer as well as to their next employer (if needed). For a long time getting an MBA has been an option that many product managers have considered. The big drawback has always been the amount of time that this degree requires on top of all of your other responsibilities. It turns out that there is another option: the executive MBA.

I guess a good question to start off with is how does an executive MBA differ from a "regular" MBA? An executive MBA generally meets every other weekend for two full days – Friday and Saturday. Students generally travel to campus to participate in classes. While not in class, remotely located students collaborate to complete class assignments.

There's also the issue of time: an executive MBA generally takes two years from start to finish. If you are working and choose to participate in a regular MBA, there's a good chance that it will end up taking you longer to complete your degree as you take one or two classes a semester.

Where to go is the big question if you choose to pursue an executive MBA. There are a lot of executive MBA programs out there and because they are such a profit center for universities, they are all marketed heavily. Thankfully the folks over at the Wall Street Journal have taken the time to conduct a survey and they've found the best places for a product manager to go if you choose to get this type of degree.

Just how do you go about ranking executive MBA programs? Well over at the WSJ they decided to go about doing it based on multiple criteria. The most important factor that they chose was how corporations viewed the programs – I mean you're really getting the degree to boost your marketability, right? Next came how students in the program actually felt about the program. Finally, the value of what they were being taught was factored in.

So who won? Here's the ranking of the top 10 executive MBA programs as computed by the Wall Street Journal:

1. Northwestern University (Kellogg)
2. University of Pennsylvania (Wharton)
3. Thunderbird School of Global Management
4. University of Southern California (Marshall)
5. University of North Carolina (Kenan-Flagler)
6. University of Michigan (Ross)
7. Cornell University (Johnson)
8. Columbia University (NY Program)
9. University of Chicago
10. Duke University (Fuqua)

So what do YOU need to consider if you are thinking about enrolling in an executive MBA program above and beyond which program ranks the highest? One interesting point is just how much this is going to cost.

The executive MBA programs that were reviewed by the Wall Street Journal cost between $65,000 and $160,000 just in tuition (books, travel, etc. would all be extra). Since lots of students work for firms that pay all/part of the cost of the program, the median out-of-pocket cost turned out to be something like $45,000. Of course then there's the issue of travel...

In the survey, 64% of the executive MBA students traveled less than 50 miles to go to school which means most of them are local to the school. However 7% traveled up to 200 miles and 9% traveled more than 1,000 miles.

In the end, the big question is if this is all worth it? Once again we can go back to the survey to find out. 24% of those students surveyed said that they had been given a both a raise and a promotion since they started executive MBA classes. Another 30% said that they expect both in the next year.

Chapter 11

The Product Manager's Reading List

The Product Manager's Reading List

Congratulations – you are a Product Manager. Now how do you stay on top of your profession? We all know that the world keeps changing and the skills and talents that it takes to be a product manager keep changing with it. The challenge that we all face is how do you become a better product manager?

The classic tale of becoming better belongs to Michael Jordan. Hopefully everyone knows that Michael was a powerhouse in the game of basketball. What everyone might not know is how hard Michael worked off the court. In his autobiography, "For the Love of the Game : My Story", Michael described how he got up early to run, did countless pushups, trained with weights and did more than everyone else in order to be as successful as he was.

As a product manager you need to do the same. However, no running is involved. Instead, you need to be constantly reading and studying in order to be taking in new ideas and understanding what works and doesn't work in the world of Product Management. To help you with this task, I proudly present the Product Manager reading list. It's not perfect, it's not complete, but it's a good start for every product manager:

1. **The Wall Street Journal**: Read it cover to cover every day. This is what the rest of the business world is reading and so you need to read it just to keep up with them.

2. **The Harvard Business Review**: it can be a tough read and it's fairly expensive, but this is what your CEO is reading. It's got BIG ideas and these can help you to understand how to fix things that are fundamentally wrong in your department.

3. **The Economist**: This is just good reading. It turns out that your product is affected by events that are occurring in the rest of the world. This is where you'll find out about them first. Oh, and it's a British

publication so they spell things funny.

4. **The Innovator's Dilemma**: This is the classic text that explains how new technology can come along and knock a solid, well established product off of its perch and make it vanish. It's a must read for all product managers.

5. **Kotler on Marketing: How to Create, Win, and Dominate Markets:** Philip Kotler pretty much walks on water when it comes to marketing. Everyone who is anyone comes to him to ask for advice. In this book he lays out his thoughts on how to market your products successfully in the modern world. Once again, a must read for product managers.

Chapter 12

Internet Job Hunting Tips For Product Mangers

Internet Job Hunting Tips For Product Mangers

In these tough times, even Product Mangers may find themselves out on the street looking for a new job. Within the product manager community there has been a fast moving discussion about what to do when you find yourself "between jobs". One topic that has not been dealt with has been what **Internet job boards** work best for product mangers?

It turns out that there are currently over **60,000 different job boards** on the Internet. What this means is that there are way too many for you to search all of them. Looks like you are going to need some help in narrowing down your search.

The Big Boys

Let's start out with the ones that everyone knows (because of Superbowl ads): Monster.com and CareerBuilder.com. The job search experts pretty much all agree on these ones: they are actually a good place to go looking if you are a **young person looking for an entry level job**. The older you are and the more experience you have, then you'll want to look elsewhere.

What Job Boards Should I Be Looking At?

Here's a quick list:

- **Jobbing.com** – good for local employment, covers 41 metro areas, has staff that physically goes and meet with professional associations to talk about how to get hired.

- **Jobcentral.com** – passes you right through to the web site of the firm that is posting the job so you know that your information will get to the right people.

- **Craigslist.com** – you know it, you love it. Surprisingly enough this is one of the most open / transparent sites out there. Be careful though, it's easy to start a scam and so don't reveal too much too early.

- **Execunet.com** – it's a serious job site that really does a good job of cutting down on the noise and focusing on the jobs that are available.

Should You Pay To Get Access To Job Postings?

Some sites, like TheLadders.com and Execunet.com charge a fee if you want to respond to a job posting. Are they worth it? The answer seems to be yes. You don't really have to pay too much and you seem to **get access to good solid job postings**. You will need to be careful because once you have paid to access the sites, they will keep trying to sell you upgrades and more features.

Any Final Words?

You already know what I'm going to say – job boards of any type are not the ideal way for you to find your next job. The key is to get out there and **network like there is no tomorrow**. Remember, they say that 70% of jobs that get filled were never advertised!

Hard work does not
guarantee success;
However, success does
not happen
without hard work.

- Dr. Jim Anderson

Create Products Your Customers Want At A Price That They Are Willing To Pay!

Dr. Jim Anderson is available to provide training and coaching on the two topics that are the most important to product managers everywhere: how do I create the products that my customers want and what should I price them at?

Dr. Anderson believes that in order to both learn and remember what he says, product managers need to laugh. Each one of his speeches is full of fun and humor so that what he says "sticks" with everyone.

Dr. Anderson's Product Management Training Includes:

1. How can you segment your market?
2. What problems are your customers having right now?
3. Which of your customer's problems does your product solve?
4. How much of this problem does your product solve?
5. How much will it cost your customer if they don't fix this problem?

Dr. Jim Anderson presents over 100 speeches per year. To invite Dr. Anderson to speak at your event, contact him at:

Phone: 813-418-6970 or
Email: jim@BlueElephantConsulting.com

Photo Credits:

Cover - By: Jason Major

 http://www.flickr.com/photos/lightsinthedark/

Chapter 1 - By: teakwood

http://www.flickr.com/photos/teakwood/

Chapter 2 - By: Serge Melki

http://www.flickr.com/photos/sergemelki/

Chapter 3 - By: William Grootonk

http://www.flickr.com/photos/catatronic/

Chapter 4 - By: THE 1 SECOND FILM

http://www.flickr.com/photos/the1secondfilm/

Chapter 5 - By: Madeline Wright

http://www.flickr.com/photos/madaroni/

Chapter 6 - By: kylebaker

http://www.flickr.com/photos/kylebaker

Chapter 7 - By: Toni Verdú Carbó
http://www.flickr.com/photos/tonivc/

Chapter 8 - By: reway2007
http://www.flickr.com/photos/reway2007/

Chapter 9 - By: Timothy Krause
http://www.flickr.com/photos/timothykrause/

Chapter 10 - By: Mays Business School at Texas A&M University
http://www.flickr.com/photos/maysbusinessschool/

Chapter 11 - By: Mo Riza
http://www.flickr.com/photos/moriza/

Chapter 12 - By: macbros
http://www.flickr.com/photos/macbros/

www.ingramcontent.com/pod-product-compliance
Lightning Source LLC
Chambersburg PA
CBHW071645170526
45166CB00003B/1441